T0353687

Dreams and Shadows

JAMES T. DOMINICUS

BALBOA.PRESS
A DIVISION OF HAY HOUSE

Balboa Press books may be ordered through booksellers or by contacting:

Balboa Press
A Division of Hay House
1663 Liberty Drive
Bloomington, IN 47403
www.balboapress.com
844-682-1282

Because of the dynamic nature of the Internet, any web addresses or links contained in this book may have changed since publication and may no longer be valid. The views expressed in this work are solely those of the author and do not necessarily reflect the views of the publisher, and the publisher hereby disclaims any responsibility for them.

The author of this book does not dispense medical advice or prescribe the use of any technique as a form of treatment for physical, emotional, or medical problems without the advice of a physician, either directly or indirectly. The intent of the author is only to offer information of a general nature to help you in your quest for emotional and spiritual well-being. In the event you use any of the information in this book for yourself, which is your constitutional right, the author and the publisher assume no responsibility for your actions.

Any people depicted in stock imagery provided by Getty Images are models, and such images are being used for illustrative purposes only.
Certain stock imagery © Getty Images.

Print information available on the last page.

ISBN: 979-8-7652-3274-3 (sc)
ISBN: 979-8-7652-3275-0 (e)

Balboa Press rev. date: 08/10/2022

"Plain English"

My girl, gone, gone away 'til Tuesday
You claim to have the magical powers of expression
But never show up
And my girl towers over you
A trust in a fund grows
My money for the broke goes broker
I cry, "it's just a little more"
Waisted on the divine queen of capitol
A dog in my blanket
An empty park with no one
Those are my days
Where's my April I screamed
On deaf ears, turbulent no one saw
And the what could happen tomorrow
Is in a closet
The sprinklers come on
The sun lives in the sky
To the point, I am sad
Plain English
Oblique, no future
Am I in the dark?

I don't want to be in the backyard
I don't want to dream blind
What I can't have, what I can't get
Just another day to be sad
And the wind blows
And I call bullshit
All the things in front of me are dead answers
It's not anything difficult
It's not complex
It's plain english

1

"IQ 132"

But it's higher than that
I can climb so high
I can see the valley and the peaks
When there's a little bit left
You can find me
I'm the looking glass
I see a Rimbaud
I'm the counter culture clash
It's haunted me all my life
That you didn't get to grow up
Your words are mine
One in the same
I miss my brother
I miss the artist that never was
My ever sense, my poetic battle
Him, me that the inconsequential
Would be born with a new meaning
I'm two shades blue
One away from you
I own the right to my own relevance
I never gave hope
I never gave promise
That you would think for one second
That I was capable of these words
If you like what you got don't ditch it
If you like what have don't throw it away

Enough said?

"Water bomb"

I never get what I want
So that's it, that's all I get
I wanna be alive
I wanna be valued, desired
Vast is the sea
And few are the fish
I called to the dog
She crossed the street with me
Beautiful Nova, white dog with sky blue eyes
My strength is gone, somewhere else
I'm vacant, a candy melting in the sun
Granulated on my brain
Cutting flowers for you
Making the time go by for you
Lonely streets and abundant heat
Poltergeist energy
Going down my arms
Lovers part and I wonder
What it would be like
To love again

"Blue lava"

Looking at heaven
A car that goes by
Beautiful woman abound
And alone is who I am
Another cigarette in the gutter
Another dream that fades away
I want and desire
With nothing to show
It should be rewrote

Looking at heaven
With nothing to show

And I am beside what is lovely
A little bestowed
Tiny inclinations of yeah
And then the thunder crashes

"Blue lava and Brisbane"

On a river
Just the other day
I had thoughts of suicide
A mimic in my mind
Where to go, who to kill
Just wiping clean
A thought, a memory
Words appear
Then recede
A victim of failure
Dancing with a hot dog

It has work
To use it
And I am not going to
Yesterday
The past
Came crashing down
I looked through the window
A million of them to see
But none for me
Wrong size, wrong shape
I gave up and held on
To what I have

"Ha ha grandpa"

Feet in the gutter
Dog in the backyard
On the streets
Begging for some heat
Give me a shake
Move it round
Show me what you got
A lil show for my eyes
My key to today
Never showed up
Lonely and the wind goes on
Trapped in malevolent society
Someone let me out
The bars are cold
My broken I am
Turned to diamonds
No one sees
In the devils gut
I claw to find a window
Let me out of hell
Breath with me
Let it come

"Serapeum"

What the fuck?
Everyone disappears
And I get pissed off

How many
How long
And I get nothing

So what the fuck
I'm not a playboy
To be fucked by you

"In your ass"

I wanna cum
In your ass
I wanna lick
In your ass
I wanna feel strong
In your ass
I wanna scream, "fuck!"
I'm your ass

"Cream dejourne"

I'm the night time
My middle and ring finger
Reveal a V to me
Sat on the bottom

Breath of life
A man with bags of bottles
And his V
Then he's gone

From the streets
Aptitude and polarity
Brush a dim napkin
Darker, darker, darker

Bottles on the ground
Spilt orange soda
Mexicans and music
Orange cones come alive

Here today we play
Faux very fold tomorrow
Fancy in our midst
Old and precluded

Read the mountain of paintings
Hi adrift imagination
Call her down the steps
To allude compliment

Burning hot on the altar
Where no God can recognize
Loyalty in a barrel
Just a little surmise

"Unsolicited"

Brittle and unearthed
Dig my bones up
Sending mud pies to nowhere
Where the lazy man curses
Interaction in upheaval
Denied your hearts desire
A vampire with roses
And no one to give them to
Vampires are strangers
That no one will ever know
Neglected and unfashioned on a chain
Where the blood flows backwards
It's not hard to find me
My heart bleeds
With pressure building in my soul
Bitten by anxiety
My bones are red
My introduction fell on deaf ears
I wanted to to die

"The repentant heart seeking a jewel"

I flailed in poetic utterance
"Come to me!"
My lucky stance an offense
Beauty where are you
As my dreams die on a fence post
An injustice done to me
As I changed my thoughts in solitude
A brow and a wink absent
The goods and not knowing
As years pass me in all direction
The son of a butcher, a devil!-
Is where I lie
Cognitive and unscathed
The heart beats captive
In a glass box with a red sheet draped over it
Blind to the feel, deaf to the touch
Alone in the barrow I ache
Dig up my bones and animate my gesture
That I drink in a bar
Not too far from home
7/28/22

"One of the two"

In gratitude and understanding
I took your hand
We played and laughed
And I attempt to recapture that

Days I don't count
Turn to years alone
It feels absolute and incomplete

As if impossible
I cling to one final hope

That you'll be there

"Dragoi"

The part of me
That bends as a bow
Refining light eyes
Straight and narrow
Cut to the chase and brilliant
My eye, my heart burn in a fire
Looking at you I judge your value
Abated and trashed
There's nothing to pick up
Maybe in these words
I can find a narrow slot
To fit my bow

Depression as a stake in the ground
Thoughts and nakedness before my only love
Youth and beauty evade me
Strange looks and no gazes
A dream that I can't hold
Tomorrow has no promises
And I plead for rejuvenation

"It burns in hell"

Sick and abated I am dead
The unnatural and other do not smile at me
I am rejected everyday in some way
Looking for one pretty flower
The rose bushes scathe at my glance
Words like power drip from my veins
And the busy faces-I found none
The years like cold walls disable me
In chains my longing is a reproach
Neon liquor store lights are my friend
The homeless and unloveable are my loves
It feels like the end
And I want to die in this park
My wrist and blood flowing out of me
The darker it gets I am home
No, I am not yours to reject
I walk in death with dark around my eyes
A pale face, a disfigured glare-free to no one
Dig me up from the ground
Spit on my bones and give me flesh
Clouds vanquish the stars and moon
A fool to believe that I would be wanted
Every day is oblivion, the first chapter of Armageddon
What does any thing mean lost without you
Your face was heaven to me
But what can I do stuck in my barrow
No temptation came courting
A cool head with rockets above me
I dove in to the consciousness of submersion
Dragged me back to the edge
In my crystal line form brazen
I am the same type as I am
Something different, something other worldly
Come down my path and play
I'll strum a guitar as you dance

I'll sing as they throw roses to you feet
I slouch on the ground like an Indian
And my doggy begs for more soda pop
He cries and whines so I pour him more
The fire pit burns
And alone I meditate in the flame
I want to cling to my father
Begging an answer that it's not the end
I'm never alone with my doggy
And I hug him praying for the stars to come out
That my head returns to slumber
And my mind closes it's gates
To sleep

"Graduation"

I remember
In fire and flame
Old times that don't come back
They come and have a good time
Then tomorrow they vanish
Leaving me in vanquish
Steps appearing as
I postulate and I plead
That deaf ears only ignore
Grow me as a man
That the smallest become my embrace
I am not for you
As the hallow wind blows
Just a picture, just a nice thought
Where does the devil burn my desire
What tree and what clock will turn around
Dashing and praying I'm am unamused
Is there a time for me
A time to take what I miss and do not get
I've grown accustomed to the dead silence
I've known nothing but an empty soul
Waiting for something, a wait for how long
God and the others say nothing
Feeling damned I say no more

"Tomorrow"

In every man's mind is a universe
A vast vacuum with stars
There was yesterday, today and tomorrow
Married in sequence, capable and adrift
Time bends on the out skirts
We travel through to meek beginnings
In a bottle of words-the hearts emotion
Span a length and walking time
An onion
A bell pepper
A pyramid
A microwave of possibilities
In the air it touches and alters us
That our universe quakes
The fields and back dreams look back
Yet our forward motion is so slow
Trance like we all have it
But it is developed only by those
Who have an understanding of the other

"Bad days"

Bad days have fallen on my skull
There is nothing
And no one to talk to
Goddamned my soul to loneliness
The day is worse than all my fears
The world and rejection have stabbed me
I said good bye to all the world's stupid shit
The bar was closed so I sat outside
And waited and waited
I'm sick, malnourished from no love
The tropical rains run down my face
The retarded try to seduce me
But I am a thousand miles away
Another town calls me
Another place to drink and forget
How severe the injury of my heart is
In the afternoon I am angry
Two steps away from the edge of insanity
Busy feet take me to my end
Time is congested, the feelings gone away
Out side the Mexican restaurant and liquor store
I'm told to forget any happiness
The rain is coming, I am waiting
SLO Town was just a dream
Natural flavor but artificial color
A dead end when you look at me
Everyone spoken for
My blood dried up

"Graduation"

I remember
In fire and flame
Old times that don't come back
They come and have a good time
Then tomorrow they vanish
Leaving me in vanquish
Steps appearing as
I postulate and I plead
That deaf ears only ignore
Grow me as a man
That the smallest become my embrace
I am not for you
As the hallow wind blows
Just a picture, just a nice thought
Where does the devil burn my desire
What tree and what clock will turn around
Dashing and praying I'm am unamused
Is there a time for me
A time to take what I miss and do not get
I've grown accustomed to the dead silence
I've known nothing but an empty soul
Waiting for something, a wait for how long
God and the others say nothing
Feeling damned I say no more

"Tomorrow"

In every man's mind is a universe
A vast vacuum with stars
There was yesterday, today and tomorrow
Married in sequence, capable and adrift
Time bends on the out skirts
We travel through to meek beginnings
In a bottle of words-the hearts emotion
Span a length and walking time
An onion
A bell pepper
A pyramid
A microwave of possibilities
In the air it touches and alters us
That our universe quakes
The fields and back dreams look back
Yet our forward motion is so slow
Trance like we all have it
But it is developed only by those
Who have an understanding of the other

"And then"

Do you remember
In the sun lit days
Our words
And then a fuck
You came over and over
Until I bbqed all over the place
Then it was real
Then it was staunch
And words became reality
That when you cum
That's me making it happen
Dreams like dragon tails
Old men remember
The memory fading into back light
Just one more day
To recognize and steal
The unattainable

"How to"

Start a real life conversation
Establish a line of communication
It's not hard
But for some there's no appeal

I am not a blank
I am in color like fruit
Take me with you
Real and pretty for today

You stupid little bitch
What the fuck!
I got no time for interruptions
I'm on fire

So talk to me
Light me up with words
Give me your dreams
Give me that I am nonetheless

I'm a stereo tuned down
A bright star with a mean gaze
Born to be thrown away
Impolite and so bold

Where will today go
And who will come along
I'm your man, all day, all night
So let us indulge

"Coming of fairy"

She came out in a dress
And damn those legs stretched
Like the inshore
Long beaches and tight fill her ups
Lust unabashed clashing
Like her high tide
Come crashing in
And in
Today might as well
Be her birthday
Dressed all fancy
Skirt to kill
Polite eyes to know our steps
Damn
I love you

"Ok, I'll drive"

Repository and no spite
Young and challenged
Put it where no belongs
Lost in the words
Turn a negative into a positive
The ever greens on Cox lane
A house ticking with time
The fish that bit
Lost in the grass
My cigarette tumbles
Everything's so simple
And stupid

"Stupid and bullshit"

Something open up a gateway
Let me through
To the other side
Looking but what does it all mean
Confused and broken hearted
For six years without a go
Everything is somebody else's
Am I so unattractive
To be alone
I'm invisible to you
Every day get what you deserve
I curse and replenish the drought
I feel so worthless and abashed
Nothing happens, nothing comes
Does it help that I tore the page out

"Love and sex"

Punish my anxieties
Focus my minuscule vision
Come to my bed
Let the A bombs drop
What the poor boy gets
Rain pisses on
I walked down A street
I got nothing
Possibilities
But no one is taking a chance
Define a purpose
Just to talk to another living person
I want to fuck Carmen
I want to feel her tight

"Instigation on the run"

Contemplation in bloom
The rail road tracks turn
To stairs
Up in clouds;
The descend meeting me so
That I ascend
Leaving my shadows on a leash,
Vacant hometown
Pride

The gift of illusion awaits
On a Sunday morning
Quiet inside
Warmth is received, analytical
Bathing
Trees and brick
Walls, the fall of eyes
To the ground! A little
Thought, your kiss
Then hopeless cycles ensue

"Black"

Black and bleak, I watch
Myself trade
Places with my shadow
The cold creeps in, the pours
Of my skin hardening and
Moisture cannot extract the
Dry thoughts
Counter act, make claim
In files
And put a stamp to mail it
The civil war of my own
Soul is exhausting
Battles away
Resume
On Sunday

"Angel hair"

I was so happy, for two days I had a temporary girlfriend. Everything of a three month existence was there, crammed for my delight, but hers I'll never know. There was lunch on the dock by the rock, it rained outside on the sea. Memory never far of that rock and someone else. I was distracted for a time, though in the same town of a ghost, same hill, and she was a stranger.

"Phantom"

Phantoms of the skeleton ring
Dance in ceremony
Opening black eye sockets
Piercing a fire with the
Moonlight of a harvest ritual
The maidens of death
Dash they're dresses against
The ground, dust rising up
Meeting smoke
Appear in the faces that
Ritualist once wore
Foreign tongues of many
Lands all sing in
Unison, coming together
To petition the earth and
Sea under the glare of Artemis
The fire becomes
Stare-well and each word
Of the poem travels up it
Each a prayer in its
Own language, but all carry
The same meaning

Untitled or "analogy"

From wind to sea
From rain to earth
Every cycle of being that is known
Travels these
From word to fire
Fire to smoke
Carrying up each letter
All word and known thought-
Few can be secret
Just before the stars fade
Water will douse the fire
Then earth after
Wind will carry the last of smoke
And the dust of faces
And the dust of faces
Who danced under the moons
Last light, to be judged
By the archer and her court

"The injury of church"

I grit my jaw
And spit
I don't make deals
With the devil
On any Tuesday
I use his own sin tactics
To spew godly filth
On fallen angels
Sleeping in a field
Clenching the black leather word
Of God, I wield my
Sword with a reckless
Liberty
The tantrum of silent
Bystanders in
Protest is no caution
Flag I heed

"Wreckers claim"

I am ordained
To live above
And so I rise without
Ever relenting
From vengeance.
I am.
And guess what?
Jesus wept.
So put that in
Your pipe and smoke it.
I am the wrecker;
The oppressor of ungodliness;
Your salvation;
A redeemed maniac;
A Pentecostal healer.
Pain is necessary
My sheep
And my sword
Requires the tithe
Of your blood.

"The severance package of life"

Chopping heads off
The bellow crest,
Smoke rising
From the spines
Disguising blood
And all it's fancy
Expense of being.
Putting bards on
Like costumes
For an evening ball.
Spanish and Viking
Will meet, headless
And deaf to the sirens
Retrieving a stab wound
Victim. Feeling
The sensual clause
In play – a different
Touch traveling down past
Generations, lovely
And excluded from difference.
Several decades
Later I was buried
With my head still attached
And never having been
Married.

"Anxiety blister"

Naked in an open field
Of your mind
As course as it
Feels

I am reduced to
Appearing as a devil.

Bells chime from the
Old church-
I panic for
My hat
And shoes-
And here
The night comes again.
Anxiety blisters away
At my arms
Cheek and bone,
As it opens old soars.

You washed my
Olive arms white,
"How pleasant,
But I rather
Remain the black sheep
I am.

"For Brandi"

For you
I owe the world
And the world now enslaves me
To grief
Having trans-scripted
Our playing years
The sand castles
By the sea
We were married in
Have become a chateau
For the haunting
Empty with only visits
From birds
Pecking at our portraits
I'm the dining hall
The thought to demolish it
With the wrecking crew
Of my foot
My heart never knew
Any cruelty towards you
And only to preserve
No, you are forever to me
The kindest wife I never took
The lover who knew me
As none other
It seems eternal
Our castle
And that your memory
In a bottle washes up
On the shore every hour
The biggest mistake
Of going astray from you

Is a constant knife in my heart
I want to find you
To make my last wrong right again
And never let go
Of your hand ever

"Stand up"

The record spins
Our boots are on
Seeing red
Never felt so good
Organic and raw
Go our feet
And the ceiling
Take it away Lyle
Screaming at a wall
Isn't it heavenly
To be AMPed
Let the good times
Flow and flow
And flow
Liquor in my gut
I'm ready to fight
Going down
The alley is our battle field
You gave me a reason
To want
And In return
I gave you a big lot

Aliens coming at me
With baseball bats
You can't beat me up
You can't touch me
I'm the son of a prince
I'm a golden rod
Dust off our brazen attitude
Fine line in the mix

Counter cultural
The day stands still
Look at it
Want it
We got all the bells
To make an old man whistle
Stand up, you bet I did
And be counted I was
Huh Ian

"yeah"

Birthing negligence
And neglect
All to see what we don't
Scribbled over epitaphs
Like a fire bomb
Carry the vibration well
Get up, stand up
Within feet, I'll take it
Watching for the next
And the next, next

Matrix in my mind
Calendars with crossed out days
All the kids gone
It is so lonely
Kids playing makes me happy
But today is a ghost town
I got wasted
Two beers and pot
Turned me in to a zombie
I was helped back to my room
Adrift in bed
Sleep it off
I'm new again

"Inside"

Inside a shelter
With walls among
The outside
The exterior is addressed
Observing motion
Through various degrees
Of entropy

"Did and done"

The disparage of truth
Held among soothsayers
The elect of in-dominant pandemic
It's a lifeless suffocation
Cut from the flow
The lily half hazard section
Bent and chewed
Who do I owe?
Not a whole lot of anyone
Is there a tide in my game?

"Question"

How do I know
Truth among
Anything
When it is
Brought to life
And invented by
The situation
I'm the moment

"Taste"

Discouraged in violence
I taste the lifeless
The undesirable
A hand down my pants
And I'm a happy boy
But she'll go on
Holding petty nightmares
At video rental stores

"Indefinite"

Indefinite
Does it call you
Young one
With soft eyes
A pantry with plush lips
Awaits
Your soft, soft forever
Pressed against mine
Is a pretty thought
And a vacant thread
Take my skeleton hand
Pull my vicious nails out
I want new ones
Your hair
Can envelope all my thoughts
When I squeeze your hand
In mine
Kiss, kiss your soft cheeks
Quite a nice
Temporary heaven

"Cold and obvious"

The only thing a Sunday is good for
Is the intense whimsical reflection
Of deep thought
I drank the night away
Coupled up in walls like a skeleton cage
The exterior of this Spanish ghetto
Was pulsating with mythological transient struggle
My head was sick and bruised
Under a shadow of illuminated scope
Breaking down with the thought hammer
Smashing pieces in to more complex dissections
Of taste, love and longing
A desire to look deeper in to
The chorus swung baton
The cold bit air is still among
I wait for the trans-logical to come
And beat leaves, flowers and the pain
Blood dried brick wall
I wish I could send thoughts
To annihilate these walls
Arrows from my eyes
Splitting cracks
Erasing what's not there
While the dead transcend
In to some ambiguous rebirth

"Sick"

I never met her
In the Spanish ghetto
We crossed paths
The whole time she was right around
The block
All this time we could have been drinking
Back behind the church school building
Down the street, out of sight
Secluded, exchanging unimportant thoughts
I would have playfully bit your shoulder
And whispered my very best Dracula laugh
I would have let you
Hinge your legs on my lap
While you looked at the stars
And talked about slashing up zombies
With a meat cleaver
We better plan for this
And it's a shame
None of this ever happened

"Loveless"

On a bar that I turned in to your altar
Your bones were lay
I sprinkled red and white
A Spanish rose peddle over
My precious little girl
I drank a Bloody Mary
That I poured with my lips

Over your lifeless frame
New skin, wan and smooth
Formed over you
Beautiful dark mystique
Eyes took shape in your sockets
Hair like midnight grew
And I smelled a perfume like incense
Rising from you

I chanted a prayer in three words
"Let her rise"
And I was joined
By the bar hops and spectators
As they gathered around
What was happening
The rose peddles
Turned to a dress
With eyes of leopards
Decorated all over
Tall high heels with silver flowers
Trimming the brim bestowed your feet
I took your hand
And we rose up in the air
The bar maiden plucked the buttons on the juke box

And we danced in the air
She's alive they shouted
In the chorus of song
I put my hand in you
And we fell back down
Down back to the end of earth
Where the waterfall of loveless life
Ends

"Left alone in the night"

A hawks eyes are burning on me
With approaching moon
Sun beating my shoulders
Searching an expired life
Locked in mystery
I look to the feel of the day
To wonder what her thoughts were
Impressions alluding to soft glances
And half smiles
A calm soothing voice
Roaming among class rooms and halls
Who knows your story?
I ask, and I am now the same
As one I wish I could find
The memory barer of a young beauty
Taken early
I wondered about one
But now who wonder about
The one I knew
It is just not fair

"Come"

Objects and desire
There are no windows in heaven
Nor door post or frames
Vampires rise
To fame and fortune
To the mediocrity in social gathering
I thought I stood out
But I was an empty face
Buildings haunted by skeletons and TVs
No TVs in heaven
Just God on the thrown
And vampires feasting
A burrito and chicken wing
I'll get sick
At 12:00 the tumbleweeds roll
Is there genitalia in the afterlife?
Click, click
On a fountain or a dick
Slanted up on the corner
Looking good
Looking fine, dressed in flesh to kill
She gives out heart attacks
Black hair, white skin
Heavens looking good
The vampires applaud
Then leave
The town went crazy
Racing aggregate
Our lord on the throne
Nods his head

"Today"

I sit here waiting
But no one comes my way
I saw a shadow, a ghost
And nothing
Skeletons underneath all quiet
The chug of bars and bristles above
Save the introduction
Cause I'll be alone
Until I get a straight shot
I'll be pissed all day
And then there wasn't
No one
Nowhere
Nothing

"Black and white"

I'm no color
You can't jump ahead
There's no cutting
Just my solitary mind
I'm the alchemist of beauty
The creator of atropine lips
Your so, it's all worthless
I no keep looking
And nothings there
Suicide on Wednesday
Rebirth on Sunday
Trying to survive
No one answers the phone

"In the stars"

———⇒⊙⇐———

I blew a kiss up to Brandi tonight. The sun was down, light still lingered cusping the hills, turning clouds pastel pink and blue, the moon in its moment. I whispered wolf up to the moon, my eyes wanted to cry but I did not. I was out on Foxen canyon, on the side of the road up on a hill, the spot before Zaca lake. I felt like going on a drive, just to wander around. Loneliness is hard, it's getting worse living alone. I feel like half a person, I can't concentrate on anything, I am incomplete. I don't want to live past this year, I feel no purpose in life, no happiness in anything. Thoughts still fall, a new poem but the same old thing, I really need something good to happen for me this year or I am pretty much done. Blood on my hands, a romantic crusade with liquor sin and sleeping pills, a new dream never to wake up from. I'll leave only my words, my heart, my everything for nothing. Moon pies are like dreams, dreams are like moon pies.

"Money"

Shadows of arms
And faces
Feet and legs
Eyes to something
Entangled in the
Reflection of paddles
Lying spat on the
Sidewalks
Motion and energy
Fused with business
Filling in space
Pushing out the sky
And lights of a lit
Pharmacy sign
The dusks kohl
Eyes are eclipsed
By all who enter
The paddle
The shadow spirit
That temporarily records
Moods, expressions of a moment
All collaborated upon

Unknowingly

"$1.25"

The moon acts as conductor
Flailing her light
As arms and baton
Raising the music of faces
Then deploring expression
From small curious
Back to meditation
The boulevard
Of shadow theatre
Host many scenes
They can be watched
From a window above
Viewed as if you were
Watching a vampire
Sucking in the
Moods of strangers
Above and across
The windows of apartments
Are just as puddles
The curtains slit
Wide open to view
A dinner that appears
Very boring
And one that
A woman only plays
A small role
In her living room

"Playground"

On Autumn mornings
There was a secret passage way
To school that me and my brothers
Would take
Sliced right between
Two houses on a block
That wrapped around to school
A little dog would greet us
At the end of the fence
Running and barking
And growl good bye
At the other end
We would emerge in to
The trees and grass
Approaching the rear end of the playground
The noise
Of children playing
Swinging, sliding, running
And battering rubber balls
On black top
It was all heard well
Before the secret passage way
But would erupt after passing through
The scent
Of the chili factory
Not far
Seemed to stain
The cool bit morning air
You could see
The smoke rising off in the distance
Traveling before dissipating
Somewhere over the river bed

The most prominent picture
Of this end of town
We're the foot hills
That traveled with the river bed
On top
Near the edge
Before the plummet below
And running far back up
Are orange groves
That are visible
And unchanged since then

"N-a-t-a-s"

Sin
In a park
Underground below the cemetery
Late at night
Skeleton children blow
Gasoline bubbles
Lit on fire by the devil
Down below the cemetery-
The furthest inner reaches
Somewhere amongst
The under passage of time-
There is a park
For those caught
In the in between
Ghouls as men
Pale and gray
Stroll with their courted dead sweethearts
By the pond
Maimed teenagers
Claimed by automobile accidents
And substance abuse over doses
Feed black ducks
A deathly expired bread
Skeleton children blow
Gasoline bubbles
That groundskeepers light on fire

"Stepping"

No day or night exist
Just a constant dark red sky
With moody clouds
Shifting colors by the hour
Green lined with yellow undercoat
Brings the most liveliest of time
The pond lights up glowing
The reflection of the sky
The hills all around
Shine with blades of grass
Blue, swaying with no wind
But it is heard faint at times
And roaring when the three moons
Cusp the highest mountain
Which is called Jezebel

For others

The Satchell on her hip hid one of four secrets
Written down, transcribed in hieroglyphs
to only be known by its owner
Beauty and abatement emptied out
Long suffering on the floor
In the sunshine colors and symbols danced to our understanding
All too long to see a tomorrow
What did she write but sticks and circles
Yet they meant so much when addressed as purposeful

Printed in the United States
by Baker & Taylor Publisher Services